HELLO BABY!

First published 2010 by Zero to Ten

© Zero to Ten Ltd 2022 this edition

ISBN 9781840897753 hardback
ISBN 9781840897807 paperback

Bébés du Monde © 2008 Editions Milan

English text: Paul Harrison

Hello baby. – (Window on the world)
   1. Infants–Pictorial works–
   Juvenile literature.
   I. Series
   305.2'32-dc22

Picture Credits

Biosphoto: 5 (Noorani Shehzad/ Still Pictures), 6 (Cubitt Gerald) 9 (Giling Ron/ Lineair), 11 (Schytte Jorgen/ Still Pictures), 12 (Heuclin Daniel), 17 (Cooper Martha/ Peter Arnold), 22 (Hellio Jean-François & Van Ingen Nicolas), 24 (Ruoso Cyril), 26 (Fairchild Michael/ Peter Arnold), 27 (Schytte Jorgen/ Still Pictures), back cover, 28 (Gunther Michel), 30 (Lemarchand Françoise).

Corbis: Cover (Bohemian Nomad Picturemakers), 7 (Hamid Sardar), 15(Rune Hellestad), 16 (Philippe Lissac/ Godong), 20 (Hugh Sitton/ Zeffa), 21 (Angelo Cavalli/ Zeffa).

Eyedea: 4 (Liane Cary), 8 (De Wilde Patrick), 19 (Michel Gounot), 23 (Villerger S.), 25 (Fotostock).

Rapho/ Eyedea Illustration: 13 (Lucille Reyboz/ Rapho), 29 (Véronique Durruty/ Rapho).

Photo 12: 10, 14 (Photo12.com/ Alamy),

Sunset: 18 (Leduc Stéphane).

HELLO BABY!

Look! A brand new baby in a blanket; a European baby kept all cosy and warm.

Snoozing baby. Shhh, baby's asleep. This baby from Burma is fast asleep.

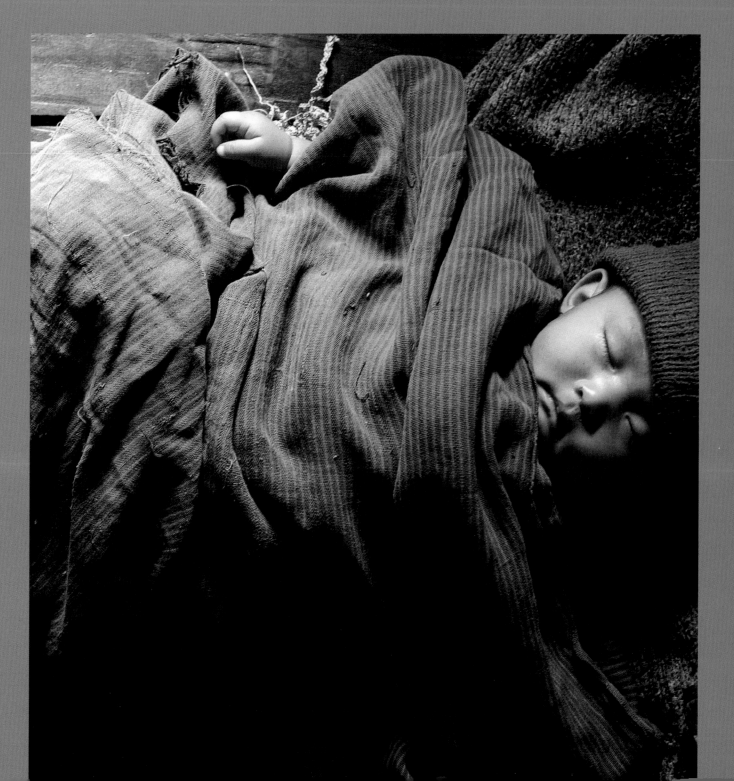

Swinging from the ceiling, wrapped in some cloth; this
Indonesian baby is being rocked to sleep.

Rock-a-bye baby in his hammock; this Mongolian baby is quiet and calm.

A hungry baby from Panama, drinking his mother's milk.
Holding on tight, he doesn't want to let go.

See the Thai baby, slurping from a bottle; drinking down milk to grow big and strong.

Feed the little girl with a spoon. This Caribbean girl is having soft, mushy food.

A Vietnamese child being fed some rice; this child has teeth and finds rice is nice!

Bath time, baby! Now for some open-air washing in an Indonesian river.

Bath time is fun here in Japan; swimming and clinging or just hanging on.

A baby in a bucket? Well, why not! This Nepalese baby thinks it's perfect if the water's not too hot.

It's fun in the bath when you are surrounded by toys.
That's what this baby in the United Kingdom likes.

Time for a check up, baby. The nurse checks a baby in Senegal - thank you baby, everything looks fine.

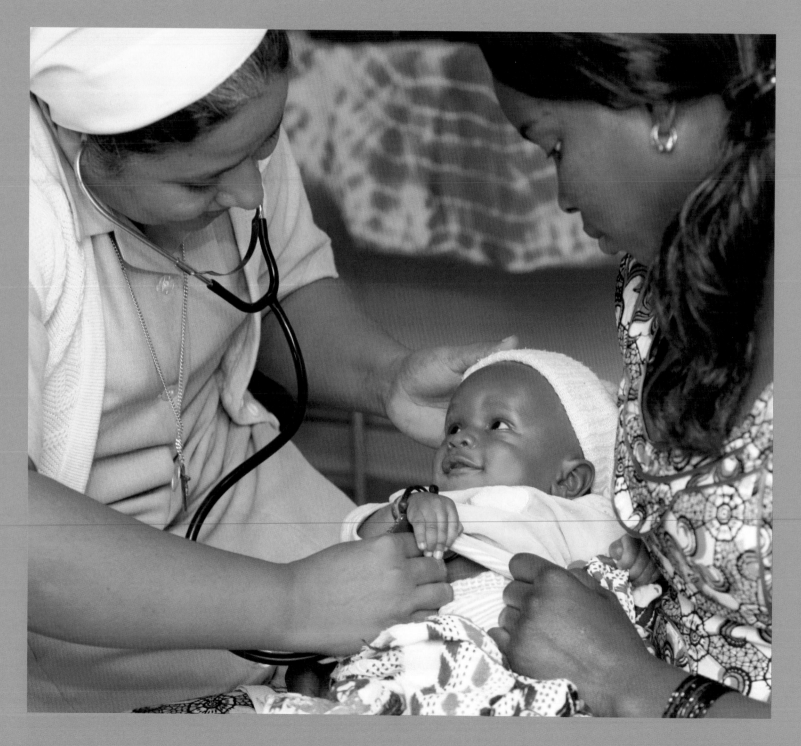

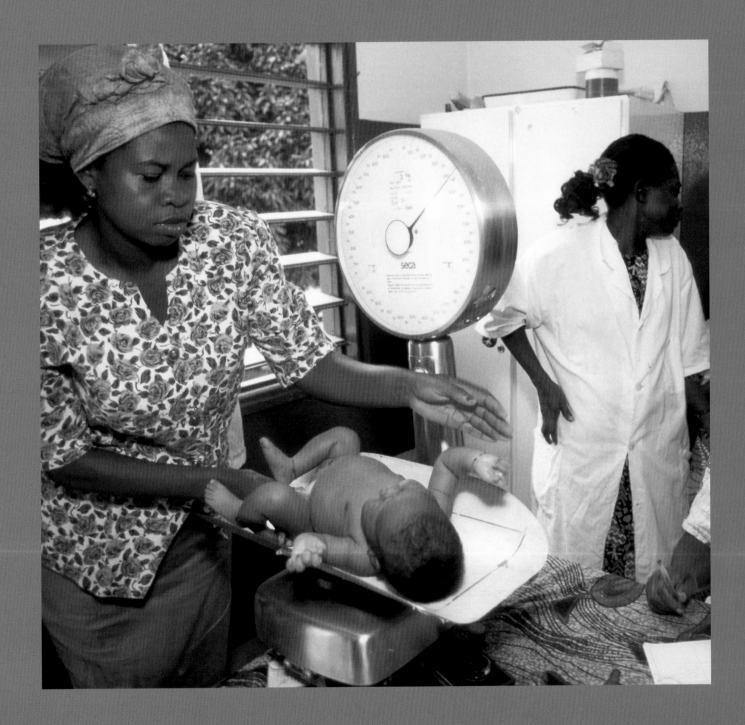

How much do you weigh? Babies grow up fast, so here in Gabon a baby is being weighed. Look how heavy you are!

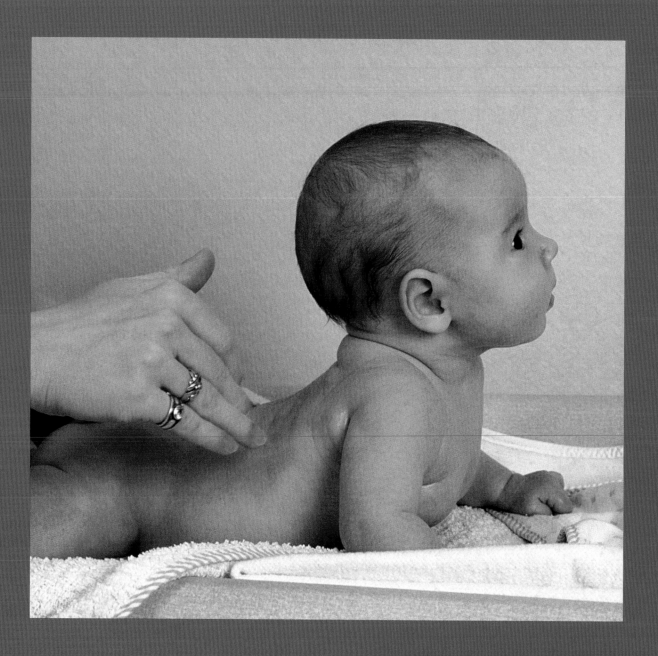

Oooh, babies love a massage! A soft, gentle rub makes this European baby smile.

In Nepal too, a massage goes down a treat. This baby is so relaxed … he's even gone to sleep!

Baby on the move; getting a ride from his mother.
This Peruvian baby is being carried in a sling.

Now here are two enjoying the view. In Burma a mother balances both her children in baskets.

Playtime baby! In Guinea-Bissau a baby scoops up soil with a spoon – it's fun to play with, but not to eat.

Peek-a-boo baby! Who's that looking back? A baby in America sees his reflection in a mirror.

Off to work! In Madagascar a baby sits in a sling while his mother works – it's tiring stuff.

School time, baby – but surely you're too young! Not in Mali when the teacher is your mum!

Come and meet the family; a Peruvian baby with her mum, dad, brother and sister.

Everyone wants to see the baby. In Niger, the whole family comes to visit this new little one.

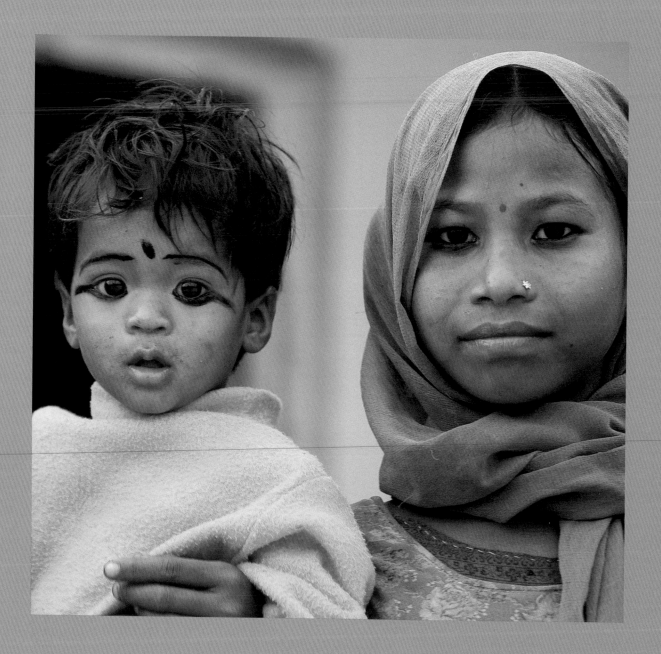

Looking good, baby! An Indian boy wears traditional face paint.

Face-painted children from Burma. The paint they use is made from trees.

All aboard baby! Chinese babies travelling home in style.

Bye-bye babies ...

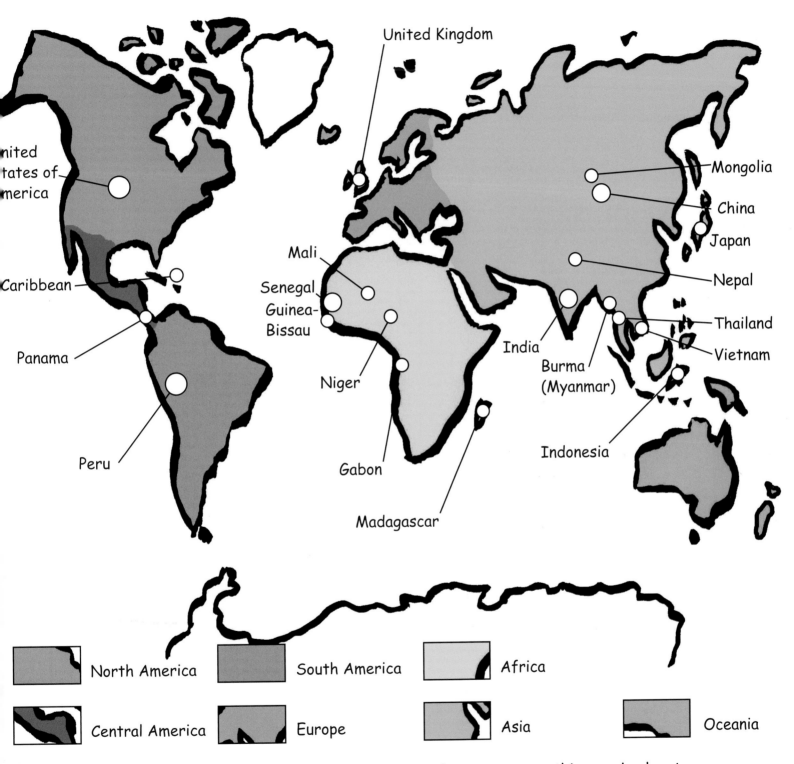

United Kingdom

Mongolia

China

Japan

Nepal

Thailand

Vietnam

Indonesia

India

Burma
(Myanmar)

Mali

Senegal

Guinea-
Bissau

Niger

Gabon

Madagascar

United
States of
America

Caribbean

Panama

Peru

	North America		South America		Africa
	Central America		Europe		Asia
	Oceania				

If you want to know where in the world the pictures are taken you can use this map. Look out
for the words in colour – they are an important clue!

Other titles in the series:

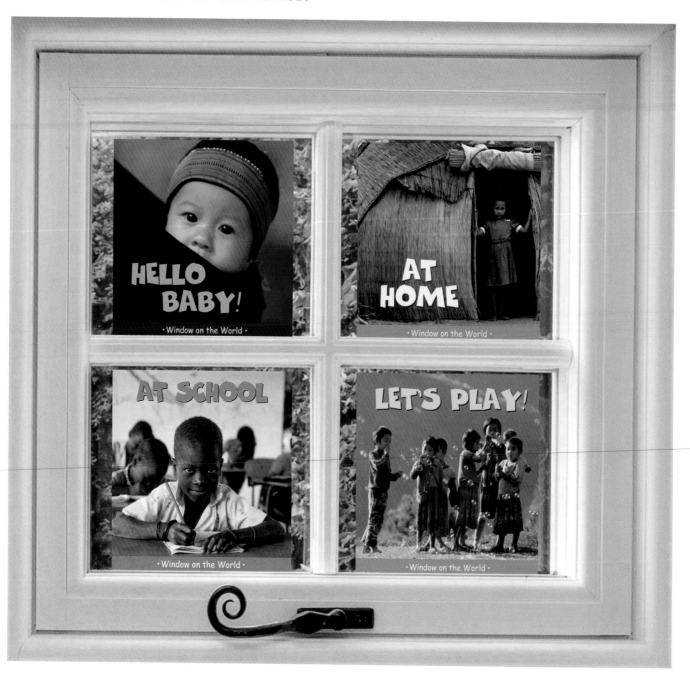

HELLO BABY!
· Window on the World ·

AT HOME
· Window on the World ·

AT SCHOOL
· Window on the World ·

LET'S PLAY!
· Window on the World ·